Silly

Easter

Jokes

for kids

Laughter is
an instant vacation.

Milton Berle

WHY SHOULDN'T YOU TELL AN EASTER EGG A GOOD JOKE?

IT MIGHT CRACK UP!

HOW DID THE SOGGY EASTER BUNNY DRY HIMSELF?

WITH A HARE DRYER!

WOULD FEBRUARY MARCH?
NO, BUT APRIL MAY.

WHAT HAPPENED WHEN THE EASTER BUNNY MET THE RABBIT

OF HIS DREAMS?

THEY LIVED HOPPILY EVER AFTER!

WHY CAN'T A RABBIT'S NOSE BE TWELVE INCHES LONG?

BECAUSE THEN IT WOULD BE A FOOT.

WHAT DO YOU CALL A LINE OF RABBITS WALKING BACKWARDS?

A RECEDING HARELINE.

WHAT IS A RABBIT'S FAVORITE DANCE?

THE BUNNY HOP.

WHAT KIND OF JEWELRY DO RABBITS WEAR?

14 CARROT GOLD.

WHAT'S THE BEST WAY TO MAKE EASTER EASIER?

PUT AN "I" WHERE THE "T" IS.

WHERE DOES EASTER TAKE PLACE EVERY YEAR?

WHERE EGGS MARKS THE SPOT!

HOW CAN YOU MAKE EASTER PREPARATIONS GO FASTER?

USE THE EGGS-PRESS LANE!

WHAT SHOULD YOU DO TO PREPARE FOR ALL THE EASTER TREATS?

EGGS-ERCISE!

WHAT HAPPENS IF YOU GET MARRIED ON EASTER?

YOU LIVE HOPPILY EVER AFTER.

WHAT DO YOU CALL A RABBIT WITH FLEAS?

BUGS BUNNY.

WHAT IS EASTER BUNNY'S FAVORITE KIND OF MUSIC?

HIP-HOP!

HOW DOES AN EASTER BUNNY KEEP HIS FUR LOOKING SO GOOD?

HARE SPRAY.

WHAT'S THE EASTER BUNNY'S FAVORITE RESTAURANT?

IHOP.

HOW DO YOU WRITE A LETTER TO AN EASTER BUNNY?

USE HARE-MAIL!

WHAT DO YOU CALL AN EASTER BUNNY WHO GETS KICKED OUT OF SCHOOL?

EGG-SPELLED.

WHAT'S THE EASTER BUNNY'S FAVORITE SPORT?

BASKET-BALL.

WHY COULDN'T THE EASTER BUNNY WATCH HIS FAVORITE SHOW?

BECAUSE HIS TV WAS SCRAMBLED!

DID YOU HEAR ABOUT THE BUNNY WHO SAT ON A BUMBLEBEE?

IT'S A TENDER TAIL!

WHERE DOES THE EASTER BUNNY GET HIS EGGS?

FROM AN EGGPLANT.

WHAT KIND OF BUNNY CAN'T HOP?

A CHOCOLATE BUNNY.

WHAT DID ONE EASTER EGG SAY TO THE OTHER?

HEARD ANY GOOD YOLKS TODAY?

WHAT DO YOU CALL AN EASTER EGG FROM OUTER SPACE?

AN EGG-STRATERRESTRIAL!

WHAT DO YOU CALL A VERY TIRED EASTER EGG?

EGGS-AUSTED.

WHAT'S AN EASTER EGG'S LEAST FAVORITE DAY?

FRY-DAY.

WHAT DO YOU CALL A MISCHIEVOUS EGG?

A PRACTICAL YOLK-ER.

WHAT DID THE EASTER EGG ASK FOR AT THE HAIR SALON?

A NEW DYE-JOB.

DID YOU HEAR THE ONE ABOUT THE HOUSE INFESTED WITH
EASTER EGGS?

IT NEEDED AN EGGS-TERMINATOR!

WHY WAS THE LITTLE GIRL SAD AFTER THE EASTER
EGG HUNT?

BECAUSE AN EGG BEATER!

WHY DID THE EASTER EGG HIDE?

IT WAS A LITTLE CHICKEN.

WHAT DO YOU CALL A FORGETFUL RABBIT?

A HARE-BRAIN!

WHY DID THE EASTER BUNNY CROSS THE ROAD?

NO BUNNY KNOWS!

HOW DO YOU KNOW THAT CARROTS ARE GOOD FOR YOUR EYES?

HAVE YOU EVER SEEN A RABBIT WEAR GLASSES?

WHY WON'T EASTER EGGS GO OUT AT NIGHT?

THEY DON'T WANT TO GET "BEAT UP"

WHY DON'T YOU SEE DINOSAURS AT EASTER?

BECAUSE THEY ARE EGGS-TINCT!

HOW DOES EASTER END?

WITH THE LETTER 'R'

HOW CAN YOU TELL WHICH RABBITS ARE THE OLDEST IN A GROUP?

JUST LOOK FOR THE GREY HARES

WHAT DOES THE EASTER BUNNY PLANT NEXT TO THE GREEN BEANS IN HIS GARDEN?

JELLY BEANS

WHAT DO YOU CALL A RABBIT WITH THE SNIFFLES?

A RUNNY BUNNY

HOW DO YOU KNOW THE EASTER BUNNY LIKED HIS TRIP?

BECAUSE HE SAID IT WAS EGG-CELLENT

HOW DOES A RABBIT THROW A TANTRUM?

HE GETS HOPPING MAD

HOW DOES THE EASTER BUNNY PAINT ALL THOSE EASTER EGGS?

HE HIRES SANTA'S ELVES TO HELP DURING THEIR OFF SEASON

WHAT DID THE EASTER BUNNY DO AFTER ITS WEDDING?

WENT ON A NICE BUNNYMOON

WHERE DID THE EASTER BUNNY LEARN HOW TO SKI?

THE BUNNY HILL

HOW DOES THE EASTER BUNNY TRAVEL ON VACATION?

ON HARE PLANES

HOW DO RABBITS STAY COOL DURING THE SUMMER?

WITH HARE CONDITIONING

WHERE DID THE EASTER BUNNY GO FOR A NEW TAIL?

TO A RETAIL STORE

WHAT GAME DOES THE EASTER BUNNY LIKE TO PLAY AT THE PARK?

HOPSCOTCH

WHAT DID THE EASTER BUNNY PUT A DICTIONARY IN HIS PANTS?

HE WANTED TO BE A SMARTY PANTS

WHY MAKE THE EASTER BUNNY SO LUCKY?

HE ALWAYS HAS FOUR RABBITS FEET ON HIM

WHAT KIND OF STORIES DO RABBITS LIKE BEST?
ONES WITH HOPPY ENDINGS

WHAT DO YOU CALL AN EASTER EGG FROM OUTER SPACE?

AN EGG-STRA-TERRESTRIAL

WHERE DOES DRACULA KEEP HIS EASTER CANDY?

IN HIS EASTER CASKET

WHAT DO YOU CALL THE EASTER BUNNY ON THE DAY AFTER EASTER?

TIRED

WHAT HAPPENED TO THE EASTER BUNNY WHEN HE WAS

NAUGHTY AT SCHOOL?

HE WAS EGGS-PELLED

WHY DID THE EASTER BUNNY HAVE TO FIRE THE DUCK?

HE KEPT QUACKING THE EGGS

WHY DID THE EASTER BUNNY CROSS THE ROAD?

TO PROVE HE WASN'T CHICKEN

WHAT DO YOU GET WHEN YOU CROSS A BUNNY WITH AN ONION?

A BUNION

WHY COULDN'T THE RABBIT FLY HOME FOR EASTER?

HE DIDN'T HAVE THE HARE FARE

WHAT DID THE RABBIT SAY TO THE CARROT?

IT'S BEEN NICE GNAWING YOU

WHY DID THE EASTER EGG HIDE?

HE WAS A LITTLE CHICKEN

HOW DOES AN EASTER CHICKEN BAKE A CAKE?

FROM SCRATCH

WHY ARE PEOPLE ALWAYS TIRED IN APRIL?

BECAUSE THEY'VE JUST FINISHED A MARCH

WHAT KIND OF STORIES ARE THE EASTER BUNNY'S FAVORITE?
BUNNY TALES

HOW DID THE SOGGY EASTER BUNNY DRY HIMSELF?
WITH A HARE DRYER!

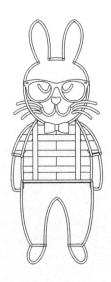

WOULD FEBRUARY MARCH?
NO, BUT APRIL MAY.

WHY DO WE PAINT EASTER EGGS?

BECAUSE IT'S EASIER THAN WALLPAPERING THEM

WHAT DO YOU CALL A MISCHIEVOUS EGG?

A PRACTICAL YOLKER

WHAT'S PINK, HAS FIVE TOES, AND IS CARRIED BY THE EASTER BUNNY?

HIS LUCKY PEOPLE'S FOOT

WHAT IS THE EASTER BUNNY'S FAVOURITE STATE CAPITAL?

ALBUNNY, NEW YORK

WHAT DO YOU NEED IF YOUR CHOCOLATE EGGS MYSTERIOUSLY DISAPPEAR?

AN EGGSPLANATION

WHY WAS THE FATHER EASTER EGG SO STRICT?

HE WAS HARD-BOILED

WHAT WOULD YOU GET IF YOU CROSSED THE EASTER BUNNY WITH A FAMOUS FRENCH GENERAL?

NAPOLEON BUNNYPARTE!

WHAT TYPE OF MOVIE IS ABOUT WATER FOWL?

A DUCKUMENTARY

WHAT DO DUCKS HAVE FOR LUNCH?

SOUP AND QUACKERS

WHY IS THE LETTER A LIKE A FLOWER?

A BEE COMES AFTER IT

WHAT DOES THE EASTER BUNNY SAY WHEN IT DOES A BURP?

EGGS-CUSE ME!

HOW CAN YOU MAKE EASTER PREPARATIONS GO FASTER?

USE THE EGGS-PRESS LANE!

WHAT DO YOU GET WHEN YOU CROSS A RABBIT WITH AN OYSTER?

THE OYSTER BUNNY.

WHAT DO YOU CALL A BUNNY WITH A LARGE BRAIN?

AN EGGHEAD.

WHAT'S THE DIFFERENCE BETWEEN THE EASTER BUNNY AND A LUMBERJACK?

ONE CHEWS AND HOPS, THE OTHER HEWS AND CHOPS.

WHAT'S THE EASTER BUNNYS FAVORITE STORY?

A COTTON TALE

A MAN WANTED AN EASTER PET FOR HIS DAUGHTER. HE LOOKED AT A BABY CHICK AND A BABY DUCK. THEY WERE BOTH CUTE, BUT HE DECIDED TO BUY THE BABY CHICK. DO YOU KNOW WHY?

THE BABY CHICK WAS A LITTLE CHEAPER.

WHAT HAPPENED TO THE EASTER BUNNY WHEN HE MISBE-HAVED AT SCHOOL?

HE WAS EGGSPELLED.

WHY DID THE TEDDY BEAR SAY NO TO DESSERT?

BECAUSE SHE WAS STUFFED.

WHAT DID THE LEFT EYE SAY TO THE RIGHT EYE?

BETWEEN US, SOMETHING SMELLS!

WHY DID THE STUDENT EAT HIS HOMEWORK?

BECAUSE THE TEACHER TOLD HIM IT WAS A PIECE OF CAKE!

WHAT DO YOU CALL A DUCK THAT GETS ALL A'S?

A WISE QUACKER.

WHAT KIND OF TREE FITS IN YOUR HAND?

A PALM TREE!

WHY DID THE COOKIE GO TO THE HOSPITAL?

BECAUSE HE FELT CRUMMY.

WHY WAS THE BABY STRAWBERRY CRYING?

BECAUSE HER PARENTS WERE IN A JAM.

HOW DO YOU TALK TO A GIANT CHICK?

USE BIG WORDS!

WHAT FALLS IN WINTER BUT NEVER GETS HURT?

SNOW!

HOW DOES THE MOON CUT HIS HAIR?

ECLIPSE IT.

HOW DO YOU GET A SQUIRREL TO LIKE YOU?

ACT LIKE A NUT!

WHAT'S WORSE THAN FINDING A WORM IN YOUR APPLE?

FINDING HALF A WORM.

WHY DID THE DINOSAUR CROSS THE ROAD?

BECAUSE THE CHICKEN WASN'T BORN YET.

WHY CAN'T ELSA HAVE A BALLOON?

BECAUSE SHE WILL LET IT GO.

HOW DO YOU MAKE A TISSUE DANCE?

YOU PUT A LITTLE BOOGIE IN IT.

WHAT DO ELVES LEARN IN SCHOOL?

THE ELF-ABET.

WHY DID THE BANANA GO TO THE DOCTOR?

BECAUSE IT WASN'T PEELING WELL.

WHAT DID THE BIG FLOWER SAY TO THE LITTLE FLOWER?

HI, BUD!

WHY DIDN'T THE ORANGE WIN THE RACE?

IT RAN OUT OF JUICE.

WHAT DID ONE TOILET SAY TO THE OTHER?

YOU LOOK FLUSHED.

WHAT KIND OF BUNNY CAN'T HOP?
A CHOCOLATE ONE!

WHAT DO YOU CALL A SLEEPY EASTER EGG?

EGG-ZOSTED!

WHY ARE YOU STUDYING YOUR EASTER CANDY?

I'M TRYING TO DECIDE WHICH CAME FIRST-THE CHOCOLATE CHICKEN OR THE CHOCOLATE EGG

WHY DID THE MAGICIAN HAVE TO CANCEL HIS SHOW?

HE'D JUST WASHED HIS HARE AND COULDN'T DO A THING WITH IT.

WHY DIDN'T THE ROBOT FINISH HIS BREAKFAST?

BECAUSE THE ORANGE JUICE TOLD HIM TO CONCENTRATE.

WHY DO BIRDS FLY?

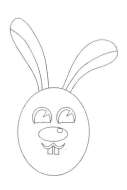

IT'S FASTER THAN WALKING.

WHY DID THE CHICKEN GO THE HOSPITAL?

BECAUSE IT NEEDED SOME TWEATMENT!

WHAT IS MORE IMPRESSIVE THAN A TALKING PARROT?

A SPELLING BEE.

WHY DO YOU NEVER SEE ELEPHANTS HIDING IN TREES?

BECAUSE THEY'RE SO GOOD AT IT!

WHAT DO YOU CALL BEARS WITH NO EARS?

B.

WHAT DO YOU CALL A FLY WITH NO WINGS?

A WALK.

WHY IS THERE A GATE AROUND CEMETERIES?

BECAUSE PEOPLE ARE DYING TO GET IN!